THE BATTLE OF THE BULGE

An Allied Victory and the Road to Liberation

Written by Amélie Roucloux
In collaboration with Pierre-Luc Plasman
Translated by Carly Probert

History   50MINUTES.com

THE BATTLE OF THE BULGE

KEY INFORMATION

- **When:** 16 December 1944 – 28 January 1945
- **Where:** The Ardennes (Belgium) and the Grand Duchy of Luxembourg
- **Context:** Second World War (1939-1945)
- **Belligerent states:** The Allies (United States and United Kingdom) and the Third Reich (Germany)
- **Commanders and leaders:**
  - Bernard Law Montgomery, British field marshal (1887-1976)
  - George Smith Patton, American general (1885-1945)
  - Hasso von Manteuffel, German general (1897-1978)
  - Josef "Sepp" Dietrich, German general (1892-1966)
- **Outcome:** Allied victory
- **Victims:**
  - British troops: approximately 200 soldiers dead, 240 wounded and 970 prisoners of war or missing
  - American troops: approximately 18 500 soldiers dead, 46 200 wounded and 10 900 prisoners of war or missing
  - German troops: approximately 29 800 soldiers dead, 34 450 wounded and 22 500 prisoners of war or missing

INTRODUCTION

The Battle of the Bulge took place at the end of the Second World War. The attack was carried out on 16 December

1944 at 5:30am by the Germans, with the aim of blocking the advance of the Allies and recapturing the port of Antwerp. For some time, the state of the German army was worrisome. Following the Normandy landings (6 June 1944), soldiers were forced to abandon the fortifications that formed the Atlantic Wall and fall back to the Western Front, unable to strike back against the Allies. However, in September 1944, Adolf Hitler (1889-1945) saw the possibility of a counter-attack. Indeed, the Allied advance had slowed due to misunderstandings, difficulties in clearing the port of Antwerp and the bloody battles that took place in the forest of Hürtgen. Therefore, Hitler set up Operation *Wacht am Rhein*, in reference to the song *Die Wacht am Rhein* (*The Watch/Guard on the Rhine*) which had an important identity value for the Germans. He wished to resume the strategy used during the invasion of Belgium in May 1940 in order to swoop down on the Belgian Ardennes, which were less defended by the Allies. The objective of this operation was to send his soldiers to seize Antwerp, cut the Allies off from this refueling source and divide their armies. After two months of fighting, the German offensive ended in failure and the losses on both sides were extensive. The massive commitment of the troops, the fierceness of the fighting and the disastrous weather conditions made the Battle of the Bulge a major event of the Second World War.

POLITICAL AND SOCIAL CONTEXT

FROM THE ATLANTIC WALL TO THE WESTWALL

For a few months, Germany experienced a strong setback. This can mainly be attributed to the Battle of El Alamein in Egypt (23 October-3 November 1942), after which German Marshal Erwin Rommel (1891-1944) was forced to leave Egypt and Africa, along with the Battle of Stalingrad (17 July 1942-2 February 1943) where the Germans once again suffered a heavy defeat. These consecutive failures drove down the morale of the German troops.

GOOD TO KNOW

The Battle of El Alamein took place from 23 October – 3 November 1942. For some time, the *Afrikakorps* (German army situated on the continent) had been gaining ground in Africa. This did not go unnoticed by Winston Churchill (British Prime Minister, 1874-1965) who ordered Marshal Bernard Law Montgomery, whose army was already on the spot, to stop the German progression. This British army was composed of 200 000 soldiers, while German Marshal Erwin Rommel only had 104 000 men. The operation was a major victory for the Allies: it allowed them to reconquer North Africa and marked the beginning of the withdrawal of the German troops on all fronts.

The Battle of Stalingrad was launched on 17 July

1942 and ended on 2 February 1943. German General Friedrich von Paulus (1890-1957) was put in charge of the attack by Adolf Hitler, and aimed to gain control of the city and thus control of the Soviet supply routes. To do this, he had control of an army of one million men. Despite these significant numbers, the German soldiers faced the violence of Russia's resistance. While the lack of food and artillery put the German army in a bad state, Adolf Hitler ordered them to continue fighting. However, on 2 February, General Friedrich von Paulus surrendered after having lost many soldiers. In total, nearly one million men died on the battlefield, making it one of Adolf Hitler's biggest military defeats.

Moreover, following the breakdown of the German-Soviet pact agreed in 1941, the USSR, Britain and the United States signed a treaty of alliance and decided to open a front in the west. With the Normandy landings, this task was completed. The Third Reich was caught between two firing lines:

- in the east, Nazi Germany faced the USSR;
- in the west, it underwent the attacks of the Allies.

The date of the landings, 6 June 1944, was yet another heavy blow dealt to the *Wehrmacht* (the name given to the German army during the Nazi regime).

CONSEQUENCES OF THE ALLIED LANDINGS

The Normandy landings

The Normandy Landings were planned for many months by U.S. General Dwight D. Eisenhower (1890-1969) in order to create a new front in the west and take control of a strategic location for the delivery of supplies. More than three million American, British and Canadian soldiers were requisitioned for the mission. At the head of this vast army was British Marshal Bernard Law Montgomery. On the night of 5-6 June 1944, thousands of paratroopers and ships stormed five beaches chosen for the occasion. In response, the Germans, who thought that the landing would be staged in a different place, showed themselves to be clueless. On 6 June, the Allied operation was announced a success. However, the toll was heavy: the Americans lost approximately 3 400 men, the British lost 3 000, the Canadians lost 335 and the Germans lost 6 500.

On 13 June 1944, the Allies filled the gaps that separated the different locations of the landings: the Atlantic Wall (fortification system designed by the Germans to prevent an Allied invasion through Britain) was pierced. After the meeting of the Allied forces in Normandy, the *Wehrmacht* could no longer contain the influx of soldiers arriving by the Channel. Harassed by Allied aircrafts, they had no choice but to retreat.

However, the Allied army also faced growing difficulties. Indeed, some Atlantic ports were inaccessible because they had been destroyed or were currently occupied by a German resistance pocket. Although this situation was not yet detrimental, as the Allies had control of a landing point in Normandy, the issue of port control was becoming increasingly crucial as the Allied armies advanced inland. This progression made supply lengthy and complicated. Therefore, the control of a port such as Antwerp became essential and, very soon, Bernard Law Montgomery was ordered to gain control of this strategic point.

Nonetheless, although the German army was retreating, it did not do so without resistance. Indeed, it aimed to buy some time in order to restore the Westwall (also called the "Siegfried Line") that would enable them to halt the Allied advance and ensure the safety of the German territory. This wall was made of natural obstacles and artificial fortifications and constituted a defensive line. Its starting point was located at the mouth of the Scheldt River, it passed through Antwerp by the Albert Canal, then a section of the Siegfried Line was located at the Belgian and Luxemburg borders, and finally it was extended through the Moselle and the Vosgas. In September 1944, after having pushed back the main body of the *Wehrmacht*, the Allies arrived in front of the Westwall.

GOOD TO KNOW

The Siegfried Line was a defensive line constructed by the Germans between 1936 and 1940. It was composed of bunkers and tunnels, as well as concrete blocks on which obstacles and mines had been placed. It stretched along the western border of the German Empire and was broken by the Allies in 1945.

On 1 September 1944, U.S. General Dwight D. Eisenhower took command of the armies. Under his leadership, the generals who played an important role during the Battle of the Bulge were the following:

- British Marshal Bernard Law Montgomery, at the head of the 21st army group, located in the north of Belgium, near the Antwerp region;
- U.S. General Omar Nelson Bradley (1893-1981), commander of the 12th U.S. army, located at the center of the Allied progression, in the Belgian Ardennes;
- U.S. General George Smith Patton (1885-1945), general of the 3rd U.S. army, located south of the Allied progression,

at the height of Alsace and Lorraine.

SEIZING THE PORT OF ANTWERP

The port of Antwerp was a strategic objective. Indeed, it was the second largest port in Europe. Its capture would allow the Allies to obtain the supplies needed for their progression towards Germany. The armies under the command of Marshal Bernard Law Montgomery were in charge of its liberation: this was achieved on 4 September 1944. However, although the port had been captured, the Scheldt estuary, which led to the North Sea, was still held by the Germans, making the port unusable. Thus, if they did not have control of the estuary, the Allies would not be able to solve the issue of refueling.

Nonetheless, Bernard Law Montgomery did not foresee the consequences and decided to attack the region of Ruhr (Germany). With this in mind, he launched Operation Market Garden in mid-September to seize strategic bridges in the Netherlands, which were then under German control. This operation was not entirely successful: the marshal failed to capture all positions and lost many men.

However, on 6 October, alerted by the precarious logistical position of the Allied armies due to their inability to operate the port of Antwerp, Bernard Law Montgomery ordered the Canadian troops to liberate the estuary. This operation cost the lives of many soldiers and it was not until 29 November that the Scheldt estuary was finally cleared. The time devoted to this mission would have unfortunate repercussions. Indeed, the Allies, venturing further and further from their supply points, had become vulnerable to a German attack. Furthermore, the lack of resources slowed their advance, allowing the *Wehrmacht* more time to recover from its recent losses. However, this mission rendered the port usable and offered a new supply point for the Allies. Adolf Hitler knew this and did not intend to give up such a strategic point so easily.

THE BATTLE OF HÜRTGEN FOREST

Hürtgen Forest is located near the Belgian-German border, in the area of U.S. General Major Josef Lawton Collins (1896-1987). This general, under the command of General Omar Nelson Bradley, showed the same eagerness as Bernard Law Montgomery to attack the Westwall. To achieve this goal, he had his troops advance towards the forest. Faced with the Allies, the German soldiers, having been able to recover from the summer campaign, fiercely resisted for many months. Therefore, the battle that began on 19 September 1944 would not end until 10 February 1945. Yet, this location did not represent any strategic interest and the dense thickets formed a barrier that should have been bypassed. In addition, the price was heavy: the Americans lost about a quarter of their men involved. Moreover, while the Allies were fighting tooth and nail for an area of no strategic interest, in the background the *Wehrmacht* was preparing in order to organize a large-scale attack on the Ardennes.

COMMANDERS AND LEADERS

BERNARD LAW MONTGOMERY, BRITISH MARSHAL

Born in London in 1887, Bernard Law Montgomery was a British Marshal. He began his military career in 1907 when he entered the Royal Military Academy of Sandhurst (United Kingdom). From 1908 to 1913, he officiated in India. A year later, he participated in the First World War (1914-1918) and left with the rank of lieutenant-colonel.

It was during the Second World War that he made history by defeating Erwin Rommel in the decisive Battle of El Alamein during the African campaign. Although this did not signal the end of the African campaign, it nevertheless represented a milestone on the African front. Indeed, from that point on, German troops would constantly be forced to retreat by the Allies. In 1944, Bernard Law Montgomery returned to London to organize the Normandy Landings that took place on 6 June 1944, which became a decisive battle in the liberation of Western Europe. As head of the 21st army division, he progressed to the port of Antwerp. He captured the bridges of Eindhoven, Nijmegen and Arnhem in the Netherlands, without liberating the estuary of Antwerp beforehand, although it was a strategic location for refueling.

During the Battle of the Bulge, he made another mistake: although he advanced quickly on the northern flank of the German breakthrough, he did not attack and merely contained the Germans' advance in this area. However, his advocates argue that this was a prudent and intelligent defense option, while his critics believe that he preferred to leave the attack to the Americans. This seems corroborated by the fact that he only switched to an offensive strategy once George Smith Patton had seized Bastogne.

At the end of the war, he continued to perform his duties in the army and died in 1976 in Alton, in the United Kingdom.

GEORGE SMITH, AMERICAN GENERAL

Born on 11 November 1885, George Smith Patton was a military man. In 1904, he entered the Military Academy at West Point and graduated five years later. In 1917 he left for Europe, but he was not directly involved in the conflict. Indeed, when he arrived in Paris, he began to harbor a passion for the tanks and decided to train men in their handling. Therefore, it was not until 1918 that he left for the front with his tanks.

During the Second World War, he participated in the campaigns in Africa, Sicily, Normandy and Lorraine. When the city of Bastogne was attacked in 1944, George Smith Patton, then general of the 3rd U.S. Army, quickly realized the urgency of the situation and, even before receiving the order, he organized the movement of his troops towards the city. Stationed on the southern flank of the Allied advance during the attack, he ordered a 90° turn of his troops and quickly advanced towards Bastogne. He played a key role in the liberation of the city and in the defeat of the German attack.

George Smith Patton died in a car accident on 21 December 1945, in Heidelberg, Germany.

HASSO VON MANTEUFFEL, GERMAN GENERAL

Born on 14 January 1897, Hasso von Manteuffel was a German general of the *Wehrmacht*. In 1908, he entered military school and he joined the German Imperial Army in 1916. Therefore, he was involved in the First World War. However, he was injured early on and departed from the front for a few months.

He soon proved himself to be one of the strongest advocates of armored divisions. He distinguished himself during the Second World War in North Africa and on the Russian front. There, Adolf Hitler noticed his qualities as a military leader and selected him to command the 5th armored division in the Ardennes attack. Despite leaving the battle defeated, he is recognized as the German officer who fared the best during the battle. Indeed, while it was up to the 6th German armored division led by Sepp Dietrich to perform the main force of the attack, it was the 5th division commanded by Hasso von Manteuffel that managed to get the furthest past the American lines.

After the war, he was imprisoned in an Allied camp until 1947. After his release, he became a member of the German parliament (the *Bundestag*) and a representative of the Liberal Democratic Party. He died on 24 September 1978 in Austria.

SEPP DIETRICH, GERMAN GENERAL

Born in 1892, Josef "Sepp" Dietrich was a German general officer. He enrolled in 1911 and participated in the First World War. However, once the war ended, he was demobilized and did not seek to continue his career in the army. He engaged in the *Freikorps* (group of civil fighters) and became involved with the Nazi Party in 1926. He then became a political soldier.

When World War II broke out, he was the general of the Waffen-SS (political elite army subjected to Nazi thoughts). He first participated in the conflict on the Western Front, and then moved to the Eastern Front. In 1944, he led the German troops who tried to resist the Allied landing. When his army managed to get behind the Westwall, Adolf Hitler appointed him leader of the 6th Panzer army and ordered him to deliver the main push towards Antwerp. This choice was undoubtedly one of the consequences of the assassination attempt that the Führer had just escaped: he did not trust the officers of the regular army. This was yet another mistake by Adolf Hitler, as Sepp Dietrich did not manage to get past the enemy lines.

After the war, Sepp Dietrich was sentenced to life imprisonment by the military court in Dachau due to the massacre of 84 American prisons in Baugnez. His sentence was commuted to 25 years in prison. Released in 1957, he continued to be in the crosshairs of justice for other crimes he committed from the 1930s to 1945. He died on 21st April 1966 in Ludwigsburg.

ANALYSIS OF THE BATTLE

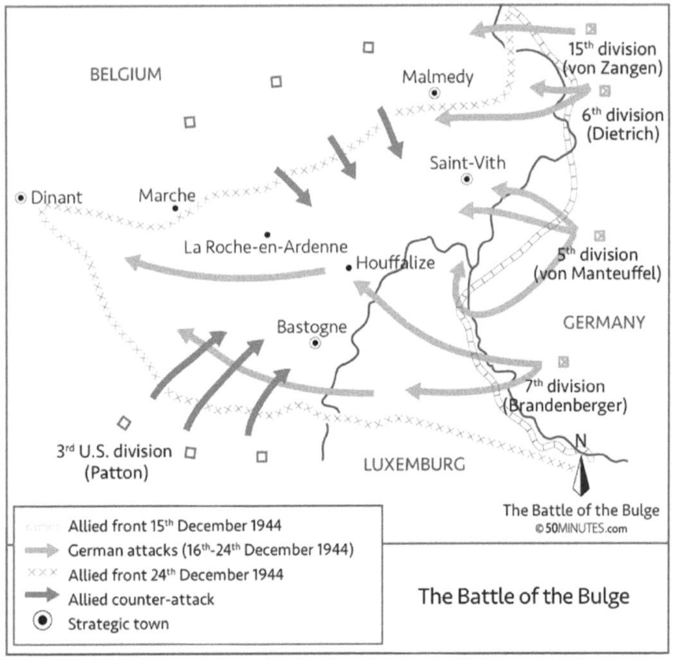

The Battle of the Bulge

GERMAN PREPARATIONS

On 16th September 1944, Adolf Hitler prepared Operation *Wacht am Rhein* to reclaim Antwerp and halt the Allied advance. The idea was to create a *Blitzkrieg* (meaning "lightning war") on the weakest sector of the Allied front: the Belgian Ardennes. To do this, the operation was based on the Manstein Plan that had allowed them to invade Belgium and split the Allied troops in 1940. The objectives of Adolf Hitler were threefold:

- to first seize the port of Antwerp and thus cut off the Allies from this refueling station;
- to then divide the British armies of Bernard Law Montgomery and the U.S. armies of Omar Nelson Bradley;
- finally, to take the Allied oil reserves, which would be useful for the German tanks that were in dire need of fuel following the continual bombing of the fuel depots.

In addition, he hoped to benefit from the vegetation in this region so that his Panzer divisions could take their positions in secrecy. Furthermore, he chose to launch the operation around the month of November, while the German army was not used to launching attacks during the winter due to poor weather conditions that made progression of the armies involved even more complex. Nonetheless, he thought long and hard before making this decision. Indeed, the *Wehrmacht* no longer had sufficient airplanes to carry out an air battle. Adolf Hitler therefore relied on the fog, which was usually frequent at that time of the year, to pin the Allied aviation to the ground, preventing them from bombing the positions of the German soldiers. The importance of this in the battle is such that the operation is also known as "Autumn Mist". It also allowed Hitler to play on the element of surprise. It was important that this operation remained secret, especially as the Allies believed the Germans to be incapable of large-scale counter-attacks.

At the end of October 1944, Hitler announced his plan to his generals, Gerd von Rundstedt (1875-1953) and Walter Model (1891-1945). However, they did not share the same enthusiasm as the Führer, for several reasons. Firstly, they considered the fact that conditions in Ardennes in the winter of 1944 would not be the same as those during the spring of 1940, meaning it would no longer constitute a favorable ground for conducting a *blitzkrieg*. Moreover, it seemed risky to them to rely on the bad weather to protect them from an attack from an Allied aircraft. They also did not believe that the *Wehrmacht* was strong enough to carry out an attack of this size against the Allied armies. Indeed, the 7th army, responsible for protecting the southern flank of the attack, was too weak and the infantry units lacked training. However, it should be noted that to compensate for the lack of manpower, Adolf Hitler launched a major recruitment drive to enlist anyone able to fight, integrating young and old people with no military experience into his army.

However, despite their reluctance, the generals were obliged to implement Adolf Hitler's plan. In the utmost secrecy, under the cover of fog and the night, the German soldiers set off towards the Belgian Ardennes. In total, there were more than 250 000 men along with over one thousand tanks, 2 000 cannons and 1 500 aircrafts in the battle. They were spread out as follows:

- In the north, the 15th army of Gustav-Adolf von Zangen (1892-1964) was responsible for protecting the northern flank of the attack.
- In the north of the center, the 6th Panzer SS army of German General Sepp Dietrich was in charge of conducting the main push during the Ardennes attack. Their target was Antwerp.
- In the south of the center, the 5th Panzer army of General Hasso von Manteuffel (1897-1978) was responsible for conducting a major push. Their target was Brussels.
- In the south, the 7th army under General Erich Brandenberger (1892-1955) was in charge of protecting the southern flank of the attack.

THE SITUATION OF THE ALLIES

Supply problems, difficulties in clearing the Scheldt estuary and the losses suffered during the Battle of Hürtgen Forest had significantly slowed the progression of the Allies. Despite this unfavorable situation, the staffs were convinced that the German army was on its knees and could not prepare large-scale attacks.

Furthermore, a disagreement broke out between British Marshal Bernard Law Montgomery and American General

George Smith Patton, who were both known for their competitiveness, over the next developments of the war. Indeed, Bernard Law Montgomery claimed it was necessary to concentrate forces on a single push towards the Ruhr region, while Patton wanted to head to Frankfurt. However, the U.S. General Dwight D. Eisenhower had the final say, and decided to operate a fits and starts advance over the entire front line. Therefore, with the main targets being the Ruhr area and Frankfurt, the bulk of the Allied armies were located north and south of the Belgian Ardennes, leaving that territory almost without defense.

This region was considered a secondary front and was only defended by four infantry divisions and one armored division under the command of Omar Nelson Bradley. Two of them were resting after taking part in the Battle of Hürtgen Forest and losing many soldiers. The other two divisions were composed of inexperienced soldiers who had recently landed in Europe. Thus, the Belgian Ardennes appeared to be a type of place for rest and the acclimatization of new units. The soldiers were even preparing to celebrate Christmas. German-born American actress and singer Marlene Dietrich (1901-1992) even visited the Allied troops on 16 December, the date of the start of the battle, only five kilometers from the front. But, shortly before, the intelligence services had warned the Allied staffs that the Germans were moving behind the front and that there was a risk of an imminent attack.

Before the attack, the Allied troops were split up as follows:

• north of the Ardennes was the 21st British division of

Marshal Bernard Law Montgomery, in the region of Antwerp;
* in the Belgian Ardennes was the 12th U.S. division of General Omar Nelson Bradley, which consisted of approximately 80 000 soldiers, 245 tanks and 590 guns;
* south of the Ardennes was the 3rd U.S. division of General George Smith Patton, in Alsace and Lorraine.

THE SURPRISE ATTACK

On 16 December 1944, at 5:30am, about a thousand tanks began the attack on the Ardennes: the attack was rapid and surprised the American soldiers. Soon, the connection lines were cut and the supply lines at the back of the front were disrupted. The Allied air force was grounded due to the dense fog. All of this allowed the *Wehrmacht* to move forward and take many prisoners. In addition, SS Lieutenant-Colonel Otto Skorenzy (1908-1975) led Operation *Greif*, which involved infiltrating the U.S. ranks with men dressed as American soldiers to disturb the order and indulge in acts of sabotage. They were quickly unmasked, but this created an atmosphere of extreme suspicion within the Allied army.

American soldiers hiding from the German artillery fire.

Everything proceeded as Adolf Hitler had hoped, despite resistance in the north that blocked the progression of Sepp Dietrich's army. The front was spread over a hundred kilometers. However, although Omar Nelson Bradley initially did not believe that this was a major attack, he quickly pulled himself together and prepared the defense. A few days later, General Dwight D. Eisenhower organized a counter-attack and decided to send the 101st U.S. Airborne Division of Anthony McAuliffe (1898-1975) to Bastogne. Bernard Law Montgomery and George Smith Patton were also called to assist. Bernard Law Montgomery, being the nearest to the theater of operations, arrived first and took position on the northern flank of the German breakthrough near the Limburg Meuse.

On the German side, the situation was complicated. Indeed, Adolf Hitler's generals' fears were confirmed: fuel reserves were depleted and it was impossible to seize the Allied stocks. In addition, the icy cold of the winter and the snowy roads complicated the German advance. Furthermore, U.S. soldiers fiercely opposed the attack. Therefore, although the *Wehrmacht* had managed to advance 30 kilometers past the Allied lines, they were late compared to the initial plan. In the north, German General Sepp Dietrich, whose role was to deliver the main push towards Antwerp, did not manage to break the Allied resistance. His breakthrough was a failure and he had to adopt a defensive position. After the initial surprise, the Allies rallied, slowing down the German advance. Moreover, the general's armored vehicles were about to run out of fuel.

However, although Sepp Dietrich was blocked by the Allied resistance, one of his officers, Joachim Peiper, managed to advance forward. He succeeded in getting close to the front from 17 December 1944 and then tried to clear a passage to the Meuse for the army of Sepp Dietrich. However, pressed by the delay caused by the German army and harassed by a group of American soldiers who destroyed all the bridges that Joachim Peiper was hoping to seize, the latter was forced to take many detours. Due to these many challenges, Joachim Peiper did not want to hinder his progress by taking soldiers, instead killing all of the men he captured. For this reason, he was guilty of the massacre of Baugnez-Malmedy and would be sentenced for it later. Finally, the lack of fuel led him to abandon his advance a few days later.

THE DEFENSE OF BASTOGNE

However, in the south, the German breakthrough was a success and on 19 December 1944, the troops of Hasso von Manteuffel arrived at Bastogne, where the 101st Airborne Division of Anthony McAuliffe was located. So as not to slow its progression, the German army decided to encircle Bastogne: this was done on the night of 21-22 December. Nonetheless, Hasso von Manteuffel hoped to seize the city, as it was at the heart of road and rail communication in the Ardennes region: it was here that the fate of the battle would be played out. Bastogne therefore represented a strong strategic interest that could allow for rapid progress towards the Meuse. Aware of this, Anthony McAuliffe refused to surrender. Hasso von Manteuffel then received the order to continue his progress towards the Meuse with the bulk of his army, leaving General Major Heinz Kokott (1900-1976) to seize the city.

American soldiers defending their positions.

Despite the difficulties created by the harsh terrain, the lack of supplies and the resistance of the American soldiers, the armies of Hasso von Manteuffel progressed and, on 24 December 1944, they found themselves at Dinant, facing the Meuse. Their objective was achieved, but success was short-lived. Indeed, their breakthrough was thin and fragile. In addition, as Sepp Dietrich had not completed his mission, the troops of von Manteuffel were exposed on the northern flank.

The Allies were also struggling to get by. Bastogne was the scene of fierce fighting: attacks were taking place day and night. The fighters of the 101st Airborne Division of Anthony McAuliffe tried all they could to push back the soldiers of the *Wehrmacht*. However, on 22 December 1944, the situation changed with the arrival of General George Smith Patton in the area of Bastogne, on the southern flank of the German breakthrough, suggesting a glimmer of hope. However, the general was facing the same difficulties as the Germans: the snow continued to fall and the access roads were too treacherous: at night, temperatures dropped to -25°C, causing significant frostbite, to the point where several soldiers needed to be evacuated. But on 23 December 1944, the weather improved and would stay that way for a few days: the fog dissipated, giving way to the sun. The aircrafts could then take off and resupply Bastogne, which was still holding up despite the violent and repeated attacks of the German army.

The situation remained alarming in Bastogne, as on 24 December the *Wehrmacht* was on the verge of seizing the city. On Christmas Day, no truce was announced: the fighting continued to rage. Therefore, on 26 December, General George Smith Patton changed tactics and decided to concentrate the bulk of his armies on one point to try and reach Bastogne. The operation was a success and he managed to break the encirclement of the city. All that remained to be done was to protect the corridor created in the middle from the enemy forces.

The return of good weather also allowed the Allied aviation to stop the German attack in the south. The 5th Panzer division of General Hasso von Manteuffel was divided into two and the 2nd Panzer division, which was the most advanced, was almost annihilated. This was the end of the German attack and the beginning of the Allied counter-attack.

THE OUTCOME OF THE BATTLE

Since the advance of the *Wehrmacht* was permanently blocked, the Germans needed to change strategy: Bastogne became the biggest target. Therefore, their goal was to break the corridor created by George Smith Patton and re-capture the city. But Anthony McAuliffe continued to resist, especially as he was now supported by George Smith Patton and his men. This was followed by fierce fighting, as well as another drop in temperatures and the return of snow. On 30 December, German General Hasso von Manteuffel launched an attack on the town that ended in failure.

On 1 January 1945, the Germans decided to launch a massive air attack. In theory this was already madness, as the Allied aircrafts were far superior in number. This failed attack would cause heavy losses among the Germans.

With the Allies having regained the upper hand and firmly holding Bastogne, the counter-attack was launched. This involved attacking the German army in a pincer movement:

- The forces of Bernard Law Montgomery were in charge of pushing back the northern flank of the German breakthrough;
- At the same time, the forces of General George Smith Patton dealt with the southern flank.

The two armies then needed to reunite. The *Wehrmacht* did not expect an attack of this scale in such bad weather. Surprised and exhausted, the German army was unprepared. On 8 January 1945, the German High Command decided to withdraw its troops to reduce the front. Some soldiers were then ordered to push back the Allies, allowing others to adopt a stronger defensive position. But the German army was nothing but a shadow of its former self and its defensive position did not last long.

It is worth noting that the Allied advance was strengthened by the rivalry between British Field Marshal Bernard Law Montgomery and U.S. General George Smith Patton, each wanting to arrive before the other. Gradually, as they advanced, the Allies discovered the horrors committed by the Germans on their way. Indeed, as its progression had to be fast, the *Wehrmacht* did not weigh itself down with any prisoners and opposed any kind of resistance with violent attacks.

American soldiers going through the woods to join the road leading to Saint-Vith-Houffalize.

On 12 January 1945, the Allies were close to reaching the junction between the northern and southern forces. George Smith Patton decided that this had to take place in the town of Houffalize, which he wanted to reach by the following day. However, resistance pockets still remained in the region to enable the withdrawal of the main troops of the *Wehrmacht*, which slowed the progression of the American soldiers. On 16 January, the junction between the northern and southern armies was conducted in Houffalize and at the Rensiwez water mill.

On 28 January 1945, the *Wehrmacht* was thrown back to the

position it held before the outbreak of hostilities, marking the end of the Battle of the Bulge and the occupation in Belgium. In the end, the human toll was heavy on both sides:

- Among the German forces, there were an estimated 29 800 soldiers killed, 34 450 wounded and more than 22 500 taken prisoner or missing;
- Among the U.S. forces, there were approximately 18 500 soldiers killed, 46 200 wounded and 10 900 taken prisoner or missing;
- Among the British forces, around 200 soldiers were killed, 240 wounded and 970 taken prisoner or missing.

In addition to these losses, approximately 2 500 Belgian civilians were killed.

REPERCUSSIONS OF THE BATTLE

THE END OF THE WAR ON THE EUROPEAN FRONT

The Battle of the Bulge was a major event of World War II, as it outlined the next stage of the progression of the Allies and the Soviets to Berlin. Adolf Hitler hoped to bring the enemy army to its knees, but the Ardennes attack mostly contributed to the weakening of the *Wehrmacht*. The losses were irreparable: while the Germans had already lost control of the skies, they were now deprived of some of their best units. On the Allied side, morale was higher than ever. They now had an even greater advantage over the enemy.

The situation in the east was no better for the Führer. It became even worse from 6 June 1944 with Operation Overlord, which was due, on the one hand, to the request of Joseph Stalin (1879-1953) to take the Third Reich in a crossfire and, on the other hand, due to the willingness of the Allies to prevent Germany from landing in the hands of the Soviet Union. However, while the Allies fought in the Ardennes, the Red Army took the opportunity to dive headfirst into the race to Berlin. Soviet soldiers finally reached the German capital on 30 April 1945. Seeing all his plans fall apart and realizing that he was defeated, Adolf Hitler committed suicide in his bunker. On 8 May, Germany had no choice but to surrender, thus ending the war in Europe.

THE TRIALS FOR WAR CRIMES

In 1942, the Allied governments decided in to put those responsible for the war crimes orchestrated during the global conflict on trial. These trials began as soon as the Third Reich had fallen. It was in this context that the German officer Joachim Peiper (1915-1976) appeared before the International Military Tribunal at Dachau in 1946 for the massacres perpetrated near the town of Malmedy. At the Battle of the Bulge, Joachim Peiper and his men ambushed a band of Allied soldiers at the crossroads of Baugnez on 17 December 1944. Having only light weapons, they were unable to resist the violence demonstrated by the German soldiers. They quickly decided to surrender and were initially taken prisoner. Later, they were grouped in a meadow and coldly shot. At his trial, Joachim Peiper was convicted and sentenced to death. However, his sentence was not applied and he was released after 10 years. Other trials followed, including the famous Nuremberg trials brought against the main leaders of the Third Reich, held from 20 November 1945 to 1 October 1946.

THE OCCUPATION OF BELGIUM

On 10 May 1940, the German troops violated the neutrality of Belgium by invading its territory. Belgian soldiers tried to fight and push back the enemy troops. For 18 days, fighting broke out in several places, but the forts fell one after another, also causing the fall of the largest cities. Seeing resources diminishing, King Leopold III (1901-1983) ordered his men to surrender. Belgium was then occupied and a new administrative system was gradually introduced. The Belgians were therefore subject to severe restrictions, particularly with regards to food; some citizens were sent to work in Germany, while others were deported. In response to this invasion, a resistance network was created, prompting the creation of intelligence services and clandestine newspapers. Moreover, many Belgians also engaged in acts of sabotage to cut the German lines of communication.

As the country's invasion took place quickly, the Belgian territory did not suffer major destruction and its factories were still functional. Therefore, the Battle of the Bulge was one of the only times during the Second World War in which Belgium experienced a real attack. The country then suffered major destruction: entire cities, communication networks and bridges were destroyed. Although this damage was not majorly disabling for Belgium after the war, this was not the case for the local people. Following the violent clashes, thousands of homes were destroyed – the towns of Saint-Vith, Malmedy, Houffalize and La Roche were the most affected. The people of the Belgian Ardennes paid a high price for the liberation of Belgium.

SUMMARY

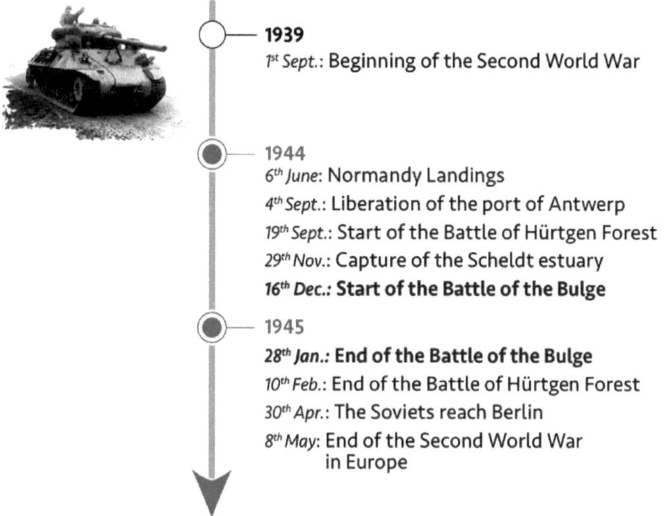

- 16 December 1944: the Ardennes attack was launched. The Allied army, completely taken by surprise, was quickly overwhelmed.

- 16-21 December 1944: the German attack continued, but Sepp Dietrich failed to make his breakthrough.

- 21 December 1944: Bastogne was encircled by the troops of Hasso von Manteuffel. Their mission was to capture this communication hub as it continued its breakthrough. This was the beginning of the resistance of Anthony McAuliffe's troops.

- 23 December 1944: the fog dissipated, the powerful Allied air force could take off and impose strong damage to the German army.

- 24 December 1944: the troops of Hasso von Manteuffel arrived at Dinant. They were at the gates of the Meuse, but the breakthrough was too thin and they could not resist attacks on the flanks as well as the Allied aircrafts.
- 26 December 1944: George Smith Patton broke the encirclement of Bastogne.
- 30 December 1944: following the inability of the German troops to cross the Meuse, Bastogne became the main strategic target. Hasso von Manteuffel then launched an attack against the city. This resulted in failure.
- 3 January 1945: the Allied counter-attack was launched. Bernard Law Montgomery and George Smith Patton sank the northern and southern flanks of the breakthrough.
- 16 January 1945: the junction between the two armies was conducted in the town of Houffalize.
- 28 January 1945: the German army was ousted from its initial positions.

We want to hear from you!
Leave a comment on your online library
and share your favourite books on social media!

BIBLIOGRAPHY

- Baugnez 44 Historical Center (No date) *Historique*. [Online]. [Accessed 5 November 2016]. Available from: <http://www.baugnez44.be/fr/historique.htm>
- Bernard, H. and Gheysens, R. (1984) *La bataille d'Ardenne : L'ultime Blitzkrieg de Hitler*. Brussels: Duculot.
- Cartier, R. (1965) *La Seconde Guerre mondiale*, volume 2. Paris: Larousse.
- Chautard, S. and Féki, M. (2012) Les Ardennes (16 décembre 1944-23 janvier 1945). In Chautard, S. (ed.) *Les Grandes Batailles de l'histoire*. Nanterre: Studyrama.
- De Lee, N. (2004) *Voices from the Battle of the Bulge*. Exeter: David & Charles Publishers.
- Encyclopædia Britannica (No date) *Anthony C. McAuliffe*. [Online] [Accessed 5 December 2016]. Available from: <https://www.britannica.com/biography/Anthony-C-McAuliffe>
- Encyclopædia Britannica (No date) *George Patton*. [Online] [Accessed 5 December 2016]. Available from: <https://www.britannica.com/biography/George-Smith-Patton>
- Encyclopædia Britannica (No date) *Hasso, baron of Manteuffel*. [Online] [Accessed 5 December 2016]. Available from: <https://www.britannica.com/biography/Hasso-Freiherr-von-Manteuffel>
- Keegan, J. (2005) *The Second World War*. London: Penguin.
- Labiausse, K. (2009) Les Ardennes (1944-1945). In *Les*

Grandes Batailles de l'histoire. De Marathon à la guerre du Golfe. Paris: J'ai lu.

- Musée de la Bataille des Ardennes (No date) *Histoire.* [Online]. [Accessed 5 December 2016]. Available from: <http://www.batarden.be/site/fr/histoire.html>
- Service de Mémoire de la Seconde Guerre Mondiale (2010) *La Bataille des Ardennes. Une chronologie succincte.* [Online]. [Accessed 5 December 2016]. Available from: <http://www.secondeguerremondiale. public.lu/fr/dossiers-thematiques/batailledesardennes/ index.html>

ADDITIONAL SOURCES

- Barron, L. (2015) *Patton at the Battle of the Bulge: How the General's Tanks Turned the Tide at Bastogne.* New York: New American Library.
- Beevor, A. (2013) *The Second World War.* New York: Back Bay Books.
- Beevor, A. (2015) *Ardennes 1944: The Battle of the Bulge.* London: Viking.
- Caddick-Adams, P. (2014) *Snow and Steel: The Battle of the Bulge, 1944-1945.* Oxford: Oxford University Press.
- Cross, R. (2002) *Battle of the Bulge 1944: Hitler's Last Hope.* Pennsylvania: Casemate.
- Parker, D.S. (2013) *Fatal Crossroads: The Untold Story of the Malmedy Massacre at the Battle of the Bulge.* Boston: Da Capo Press.
- Parker, D.S. (2016) *Hitler's Ardennes Offensive: The German View of the Battle of the Bulge.* New York: Skyhorse Publishing.

- Toland, J. (1999) *Battle: The Story of the Bulge*. Lincoln, Nebraska: University of Nebraska Press.

ICONOGRAPHIC SOURCES

- The Normandy landing. Royalty-free reproduction picture.
- American soldiers hiding from the German artillery fire. Royalty-free reproduction picture.
- American soldiers defending their positions. Royalty-free reproduction picture.
- American soldiers going through the woods to join the road leading to Saint-Vith-Houffalize. Royalty-free reproduction picture.

FILMS, TELEVISION SERIES AND DOCUMENTARIES

- *Battleground*. (1949) [Film]. William A. Wellman. Dir. USA: Metro-Goldwyn-Mayer.
- *Battle of the Bulge*. (1966) [Film]. Ken Annakin. Dir. USA: Warner Bros., Cinerama Productions, United States Pictures.
- *Castle Keep*. (1969) [Film]. Sydney Pollack. Dir. USA: Filmways.
- "Bastogne". *Band of Brothers*. (2001) [Television series]. Stephen Ambrose and Bruce C. McKenna. Writ. David Leland. Dir. USA.
- "The Breaking Point". *Band of Brothers*. (2001) [Television series]. Stephen Ambrose and Graham Yost. Writ. David Frankel. Dir. USA.

- *Saints and soldiers*. (2003) [Film]. Ryan Little. Dir. USA:
  Go Films, Medal of Honour Productions LLC.
- *Apocalypse. La 2ème Guerre mondiale*. (2009)
  [Documentary]. Isabelle Clarke and Daniel Costelle. Dir.
  France: CC&C, ECPAD.

MUSEUMS AND COMMEMORATIVE BUILDINGS

- Ardennen Poteau '44 Museum, museum dedicated to
  the Battle of the Bulge (Poteau, Belgium).
- Baugnez '44 Historical Center, museum dedicated to the
  Battle of the Bulge (Malmedy, Belgium).
- Bastogne War Museum, museum dedicated to the
  Second World War according to the Battle of the Burge
  (Bastogne, Belgium).
- Musée de la Bataille des Ardennes (La-Roche-en-
  Ardenne, Belgique).
- December '44 Historical Museum La Gleize, museum
  dedicated to the Battle of the Bulge (Stoumont,
  Belgium).
- National Museum of Military History on the Second
  World War and the Battle of the Bulge (Diekirch,
  Luxembourg).
- Ardennes American Cemetery and Memorial (Neuville-
  en-Condroz, Belgique).
- German war cemetery (Sandweiler, Luxemburg).

ISHIKAWA DIAGRAM
Material Method Machine
Mother Nature Measure Men
Management & Marketing 50MINUTES.com
THE BATTLE OF AUSTERLITZ
ADAM SMITH
Livres